# understanding
# wine labels

# Ca'del Solo

## Pinot Grigio

### MONTEREY

NON SORPRENDERE IL ELEFANTE

'A 2000
JCED & BOTTLED BY CA' DEL SOLO
CRUZ CALIFORNIA  U.S.A.
OTTO DEGLI STATI UNITI          ALC 13.0% BY VOL

stampatore tappate

# understanding wine labels

## a complete guide to wine labels around the world

2000 PINOT GRIGIO MONTEREY

Shades of the late, checkered *Domaine de Chard?* *Oh nay*! By that we mean we have a sort of interesting category mistake. This *Pinot* is actually *Grigio* - that would translate as vaguely pink within our sensory range. There is a strange unfamiliarity to seeing things as they really are. The good news is that the wine is really quite amazing. There is a wonderful *echt* pseudo-Alsace nose – there is always a dusky, jasmine, citrus peel perfume to Frenchified *Pinot Gris* and a wonderfully decadent peel-me-a-jujube-date quality that reposes recumbently in the background. Very rich with an almost unctuous texture, this *grigio* is a triumphant moment for the *Soledadese*. Please feel free to call us at (831) 425–4518 or maneuver your mouse to www.bonnydoonvineyard.com.

FIGURE

7  69434 21120  7

GOVERNMENT WARNING:
(1) ACCORDING TO THE SURGEON GENERAL, WOMEN SHOULD NOT DRINK ALCOHOLIC BEVERAGES DURING PREGNANCY BECAUSE OF THE RISK OF BIRTH DEFECTS. (2) CONSUMPTION OF ALCOHOLIC BEVERAGES IMPAIRS YOUR ABILITY TO DRIVE A CAR OR OPERATE MACHINERY, AND MAY CAUSE HEALTH PROBLEMS.

750 ML
CONTAINS SULFITES

## simon woods

### MITCHELL BEAZLEY

**understanding wine labels**
by Simon Woods

First published in Great Britain in 2004
by Mitchell Beazley, an imprint of Octopus
Publishing Group Limited, 2–4 Heron Quays,
London E14 4JP.

A CIP catalogue record for this book is
available from the British Library.

ISBN: 1 84000 846 6

The author and publishers will be grateful
for any information which will assist them
in keeping future editions up to date.
Although all reasonable care has been taken
in the preparation of this book, neither
the publishers nor the author can accept
any liability for any consequences arising
from the use thereof, or the information
contained therein.

Commissioning editor   Hilary Lumsden
Executive art editor   Yasia Williams
Managing editors   Emma Rice, Julie Sheppard
Design   Tim Pattinson
Editor   Diona Gregory
Production   Gary Hayes
Index   Laura Hicks

Typeset in RotisSansSerif

Printed and bound by
Toppan Printing Company in China

# contents

Picture the scene. Friday night. 7pm. The local store. Your basket is full of shopping and you've ticked off nearly all the items on your list. You've squeezed the vegetables. You've smelled the bread. You've checked the fish for freshness – glazed eye, no buy. And now you find yourself in the wine aisle. Just you and 800 different bottles.

# introduction

There's nothing to stop you prodding, smelling, and peering at a bottle of wine, but you won't discover much about its contents. No, the only thing that you have to tell you what to expect is that piece of paper stuck on the front – the label.

In an ideal world, the label should tell a consumer everything he or she needs to know about the wine that's in the bottle. But, unfortunately, some wine producers seem to think that their job stops when they have put their precious liquid into the bottle. In those cases a rather shabby and unhelpful label is often slapped on the bottle very much as an afterthought. At the other extreme, there are producers whose labels have come straight from a state-of-the-art graphic design studio, and that contain more information about the wine than anyone could possibly need – harvest dates, acidity levels, the name of the company that made the barrels, and more.

Given the range of wines that even the smallest of shops have today, it helps to know your way around a wine label. The more familiar you are with the various words, phrases, and numbers you see there, the less likely you are to simply stick to an old favourite, or plump for whatever is on special offer that week.

That's where this book comes in. Its aim is to help you sift through the information on the outside of a bottle and extract the truly important details about the wine on the inside. Because labelling requirements differ around the world, it's organized country-by-country. You'll notice that some countries are allocated far more space than others. This isn't a comment on the quality of the wines. It's just that labels in countries such as France and Italy can be much more confusing than those from, say, Australia and the USA.

Sadly, space constraints put a limit on the number of labels that can be shown. There's no room for a selection from Château Mouton-Rothschild in Bordeaux, which each year invites a famous artist to design a label: Picasso, Kandinsky, Chagall, and Warhol are just four who have contributed. There's also no space for the Star Trek-inspired Deep Space Wine range from Stone Creek Cellar in California – the Merlot is called Klingon Blood Wine... But in the pages that follow, you'll find plenty of other labels, and plenty of information as well. Who knows? If you get a taste for wine labels, you may even want to start your own collection and become a vinititulist.

**1973 Mouton**

The Picasso label for the 1973 Mouton-Rothschild. It wasn't a great vintage, and the wine is past its best now, but the bottles still attract those collectors who like to have a complete set of the Mouton artist labels.

You can't judge a book by its cover, but can you judge a wine by its label? Today some wine companies spend a fortune on the design of their labels and packaging in order to make their products stand out to their target market. In a wine store or large supermarket in particular, many decent tasty wines just sit on the shelf gathering dust, while inferior ones with brighter, louder, more gimmicky presentations sell like hot cakes.

# can you judge a book
# by its cover?

Does the impact of label design lessen as you climb higher up the wine price ladder? Yes and no. A reputable French producer in Burgundy which has been using the same label design on its bottles for generations probably gives little thought to its visual impact – the wine sells out every year, so why worry about it? But a fledgling producer from Central Otago in New Zealand, which makes Pinot Noir of the same price and quality has probably invested considerable time and money in the label for its wine. And while each label costs the Burgundian winemaker peanuts, the New Zealand counterpart could be paying as much as twenty pence per label.

Here are the labels from three very different bottles
of wine. All they have in common is that they are red
wines. Just by looking at them, which would you say
was the most expensive wine, and which the cheapest?

The order from cheapest to most expensive wine is Monte
Cheval Vranac, Château des Jacques Clos du Grand
Carquelin Moulin-à-Vent, Yarra Yering Dry Red No 1.
The Monte Cheval is a simple, chunky wine made from
the Vranac variety (about £5/$8.50). The wine from
Château des Jacques is one of a number of excellent
single-vineyard Moulin-à-Vents that the Jadot-owned
estate produces in Beaujolias (about £15/$25.50). Yarra
Yering Dry Red No 1 is one of Australia's finest Cabernet
Sauvignon-based wines from an eccentric doctor in the
fashionable Yarra Valley region (about £25/$42.50),
although you'd never know it from the label.

While some labels carry more information than any normal drinker could possibly want, others are exercises in minimalism and tell you hardly anything at all. Yet even these must give certain information about the wine. If you ever run out of sleeping pills, the next best thing to send you into the arms of Morpheus is a book of wine-labelling requirements. Did you know, for example, that there are rules governing the height of the typeface used on the labels? Yawn.

# legal requirements

INCÓGNITO

Select fruit from
Young vines, well
Ripened,
And hand
Harvested.

*"To live outside the law, you must be honest."* – Bob Dylan

wine@cortesdecima.pt
www.cortesdecima.pt

5 603790 001063    LIN 02 202

| CVRA | VINHO REGIONAL ALENTEJANO |
|------|---------------------------|
|      | BX 233838 |
| Dec.-Lei n.º 119/97 | DE 0,5 a 1L |

It would be great if there was just one standard the world over. There isn't. Broadly speaking, the information can be split into four categories:

## The essential

- Country of origin.
- Quality designation – requirements governing terms, such as quality wine or table wine, are different in each country.
- Name and address of the bottler.
- Volume of container – in litres, centilitres or millilitres.
- Alcohol strength – in degrees or per cent.

## The useful

- More precise details of origin – region, town or village, maybe even vineyard name.
- Name and address of the producer.

- Brand name – I'm still waiting for there to be a wine called "Travesty"...
- Vintage – a minimum proportion of grapes, usually seventy-five to eighty-five per cent, must come from the specified year.
- Grape variety/ies – forbidden in some countries, but a good indicator of wine style.
- Colour – you'd think this would be essential, but it isn't.
- Sweetness – ditto. In some regions – Alsace springs to mind – often you're not sure whether a wine is bone dry or halfway to syrup until you open it.

## The flowery

- Usually found on the back label.
- Tasting notes – can give vital pointers toward a wine's style, but can err into the realms of fantasy.
- Serving suggestions – vary from helpful ("try this light crisp white with simple fish dishes") to sick-making ("serve with good food and good friends").
- Technical information – dates of picking; sugar and acidity levels; duration and temperature of ferments; length of oak ageing, and so on. Great for wine geeks, but can confuse the novice.

## The bureaucracy

- Some countries require information on recycleability; additives used in winemaking; the number of standard drinks in the bottle, and details of the importer.

**Rules? What rules?**

In some countries, it is illegal to name certain grape varieties on the label, but this doesn't prevent clever producers from giving the odd clue to what you might find inside the bottle. Portuguese producer Cortes de Cima makes a wine in the Alentejo called Incógnito. What's it made from? Take a look at the back label (see left):

Select fruit from
Young vines, well
Ripened,
And hand
Harvested.

The note at the base of the label is a Bob Dylan lyric: "To live outside the law, you must be honest".

If all wine labels were as simple as those from the New World, then there would be no need for this book. In the last twenty years, the fortunes of New World wines – from the Americas, Australasia, and South Africa – have soared, while those of many wines from the Old World – Europe – have plummeted. The quality and consistency of the New World wines is, of course, a major part of their success, but their user-friendly packaging has also played an important role.

# new world

The biggest difference between how New and Old World wines are labelled is that, in general, the New World highlights the grape variety, while the Old World puts the emphasis on the region of origin. Familiarize yourself with maybe a dozen grapes – Cabernet Sauvignon, Grenache, Merlot, Pinot Noir, Shiraz, and Zinfandel for reds; Chardonnay, Chenin Blanc, Riesling, Sauvignon Blanc, Semillon, and Viognier for whites – and you've cracked most New World wines. As a bonus, they will often sport a back label giving further details about what to expect from the wine, with serving suggestions and maybe a pointer to a website for those who want more information.

When it comes to the Old World, informative back labels are more scarce. Meanwhile, on the front of the bottles, the most prominent words are place names like

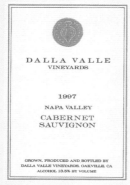

DALLA VALLE
VINEYARDS

1997

NAPA VALLEY
CABERNET
SAUVIGNON

GROWN, PRODUCED AND BOTTLED BY
DALLA VALLE VINEYARDS, OAKVILLE CA
ALCOHOL 13.5% BY VOLUME

Sancerre, Rioja, or Chianti. What do these tell a novice about the wine in the bottle? Without help at hand, how could they possibly know that France's Châteauneuf-du-Pape, Italy's Cannonau di Sardegna, and Spain's Priorat are all based on the Grenache grape?

While New World labels tend to be simpler than their Old World counterparts, is there a danger of being too simplistic? Certainly. Many people now choose Chardonnay irrespective of its region of origin, almost as if there was just one blend for the entire world. Quality-minded New World producers are aware of this, and now put more emphasis on the region of origin of their wines. Single-vineyard bottlings are becoming more common as the producers work out how different parts of their vineyards give wines with different, distinct characters. As a result, some New World wine labels are a little more wordy than they used to be, but they still have a long way to go to become as complicated as certain examples from Europe.

NAHE

1999er

Schloßböckelheimer Felsenberg

Riesling Spätlese

–HALBTROCKEN –

QUALITÄTSWEIN MIT PRÄDIKAT

WEINGUT DR. CRUSIUS

alc. 11.0% vol.  Gutsabfüllung - Produce of Germany - D-55595 Traisen - A. P. Nr. 777500901600    750 ml

**Look at these two labels**

Both are great wines, but if you were new to wine, which would you plump for? The clear and simple one, or the incomprehensible one in umlaut-ridden Gothic script with the funereal border?

If wine is now an easier drink for the world to enjoy, then we can thank Australia for that. Quality and reliability have, of course, been vitally important, but the user-friendly packaging has been just as important to the Aussies' success. Rosemount Shiraz is easy to drink, easy to pronounce, and easy to remember – a winning combination.

# australia

Many Australian wines are blends that use grapes grown in different parts of the country, so you'll often find that two or more regions are mentioned on the label – Coonawarra/McLaren Vale, for example. Multi-regional blends often appear with a state designation, such as South Australia, or with the blanket South Eastern Australia label which, in practice, means the grapes could come from anywhere outside Western Australia.

A wine industry body called the GIC (Geographical Indications Committee) is currently drawing up boundaries for the Australian wine regions. The boundary divisions are based on variations in climate and also on geological differences in the land. But there are no limits to what varieties can be planted within these boundaries, nor on the quality and style of the wines produced there.

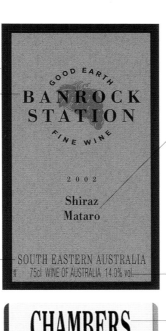

**Banrock Station** one of the many brands of BRL Hardy, now part of Constellation Wines, the world's largest wine company

**Shiraz/Mataro** Australia's most popular grape plus the revitalized Mataro, also known as Mourvèdre. The order of listing indicates that there will be at least as much (and probably more) Shiraz as Mataro

**South Eastern Australia** the appellation used for many a multi-regional blend. Quality ranges from basic to brilliant

**14%** potent in European terms, typical for many New World wines

**Chambers Rosewood Vineyards** a top fortified-wine producer

**Rare Muscat** Rutherglen Muscats are now split into four categories. In ascending order of quality and richness they are: Rutherglen Muscat, Classic, Grand, and Rare

**Rutherglen** region

**17.5%** this is fortified wine, but it's not as alcoholic as many ports

There's far more to New Zealand wines than the words "Marlborough" and "Sauvignon Blanc". A country that was once dismissed as fit only for the lacklustre Müller-Thurgau is now producing world-class Pinot Noir, Chardonnay, and Riesling (and, of course, Sauvignon), as well as some very impressive Bordeaux-inspired blends. When it comes to the labels, there are few terms you'll encounter that are not self-explanatory.

# new zealand

### Alcohol content

If the label doesn't give much indication of style, then the alcohol level can. The higher it is, the bigger the wine will be. The 1990s saw a rise in popularity of richer wines made from riper grapes, and average alcohol levels have risen as a result. Once rare, wines of fourteen per cent and higher are now common, and some monster Californian Zinfandels have been clocked at seventeen per cent!

In the same way that Australia uses the broad regional description of South Eastern Australia as a catch-all designation, so New Zealand has East Coast, an appellation which encompasses the following areas: Gisborne (also known as Poverty Bay), Hawkes Bay, and Wairarapa (also known as Martinborough) on the North Island; and Marlborough and Canterbury on the South. However, divisions are now beginning to emerge within these main regions.

In Hawke's Bay (which also appears as Hawkes Bay, depending on whose label you examine), the gravel-rich soils around Gimblett Road are proving to offer ideal conditions for red wine production. You may see a small gold sticker on the labels of some wines produced in that region, proclaiming that they are from the Gimblett Gravels.

**Block 3** not quite as romantic a sounding name as Les Amoureuses for a single vineyard, but proving to be a classy plot of land

**Felton Road** producer

**Pinot Noir** the most widely planted grape in New Zealand

**Central Otago** for many people, this is *the* region for Pinot Noir

**East Coast** the grapes for 2002 are actually all from Marlborough, but Montana has chosen to use to the East Coast designation so it doesn't have to change the label in those vintages when grapes from other regions are included in the blend – the 2000 included some Hawkes Bay fruit, for example

**Chardonnay** 100 per cent, in this instance

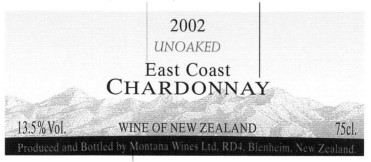

**Montana** producer

Those familiar with wines from other New World countries will have few problems with South African wines, but there are a few terms that are unique to the Cape. The country's Wine of Origin (WO) appellation system divides the vineyards into regions, districts, and wards. So the ward of Simonsberg-Stellenbosch lies in the district of Stellenbosch, which forms part of the Coastal Region. All the grapes must be from the stated area. There are also the more general appellations of Western Cape (often used when wines are blends from several WOs) and the rarely seen Northern Cape. Neither is a WO.

# south africa

Sparkling wines made by the Champagne method go by the name of méthode cap classique (MCC), while Chenin Blanc – which is the Cape's most widely planted grape – is sometimes also called Steen. The term "estate" also has an official meaning in South African wine law. Only wines made from grapes grown and vinified on the property in question can claim estate status.

Confirmation that a wine meets all these regulations appears in the form of a Wine and Spirit Board seal on the neck of the bottles. Only around a third of all South African wines are submitted for such certification. However, the majority of bottles that have been produced for export will be put forward for certification.

**Graham Beck** one of the Cape's foremost sparkling wine producers

**Méthode Cap Classique** the designation for bottle-fermented sparkling wine

**Brut** dry

**Pinot Noir/Chardonnay** the varieties, or as the South Africans say "cultivars" (short for "cultivated varieties") used

**A344** an official identity code identifying the producer. Useful for tracing the provenance of some retailer own-label wines

**Wines of Western Cape** not a WO, just a geographical area. Some other Graham Beck wines are WO Robertson

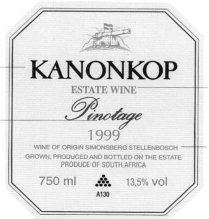

**Kanonkop** for many, the premier Pinotage producer

**Pinotage** the Cape's very own grape, a crossing of Pinot Noir and Cinsault

**Estate Wine** all the grapes are from Kanonkop's vineyards

**Wine of Origin** Simonsberg Stellenbosch is the ward where the winery and its vineyards lie

North America was the first New World country to embrace the concept of varietal wines. The craze began with Cabernet Sauvignon and Chardonnay, but now includes a range of varieties.

# north america

The varietal is a main factor in most people's choice of American wines, but there's growing interest in the origin of wines. There are nearly 150 American Viticultural Areas (AVAs), some covering vast areas and several wineries, others just one or two producers. Their boundaries are geographical or political. The term AVA doesn't have to appear on a bottle, but if it is used, then at least eighty-five per cent of the grapes must come from that region.

American back labels are among the most prosaic (and pretentious) you'll find. But two items are common to all. First, the phrase "contains sulfites". Most wines are made with the help of sulphur dioxide, but the warning is for acute asthmatics and others with respiratory problems.

Second, the government warning that women should not drink alcoholic beverages during pregnancy and that consumption of alcohol impairs the ability to drive a car or operate machinery, and may cause health problems. There is a move to counter this by promoting the health benefits of moderate wine drinking. In the future, bottles may show the message: "We encourage you to consult your family doctor about the health effects of wine consumption".

Ridge top-class producer

**RIDGE 1997**
**CALIFORNIA**
**MONTE BELLO**®

Monte Bello for Ridge, the name of the vineyard is more important than the grapes used

MONTE BELLO VINEYARD: 85% CABERNET SAUVIGNON,
8% MERLOT, 4% PETIT VERDOT, 3% CABERNET FRANC
SANTA CRUZ MOUNTAINS    ALCOHOL 12.9% BY VOLUME
PRODUCED AND BOTTLED BY RIDGE VINEYARDS, INC.    BW 4488
17100 MONTE BELLO ROAD, P.O. BOX 1810, CUPERTINO, CA 95015

Santa Cruz Mountains the AVA where the Monte Bello Vineyard lies

85% Cabernet, 8% Merlot, etc. the precise make-up of the wine. Ridge's back labels contain even more information about the wine

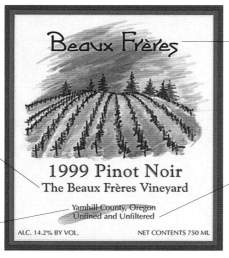

Beaux Frères

**1999 Pinot Noir**
The Beaux Frères Vineyard

Yamhill County, Oregon
Unfined and Unfiltered

ALC. 14.2% BY VOL.        NET CONTENTS 750 ML

Beaux Frères the producer. It's French for brothers-in-law, and one of the brothers-in-law who own the winery is the famous wine critic Robert Parker

The Beaux Frères Vineyard no bought-in grapes, in other words

Yamhill County, Oregon premier Pinot Noir country

Unfined and Unfiltered the winemakers have tried to make the wine as naturally as possible. Don't be surprised if there is some sediment

In Argentina and Chile there's a big difference between wines for the home market and those for export. Occasionally, the name is the same, but what's in the bottle is quite different.

# south america

### Chile

Although the range is expanding, Chile is still dominated by the big four varieties – Cabernet Sauvignon, Merlot, Chardonnay, and Sauvignon Blanc. When trying Sauvignon Blanc, keep in mind that it can be made from inferior Sauvignonasse, and that many "Merlots" contain Carmenère, an interesting, but quite different grape. Regional specialities are recognized – Chardonnay and Sauvignon Blanc from Casablanca, Merlot from Colchagua, Cabernet Sauvignon from Maipo – but the producer's name is still the most important factor on a Chilean label.

### Argentina

A wider variety of grapes are grown in Argentina. As well as the familiar French varieties, Spanish immigrants brought Tempranillo and (probably) the spicy Torrontés, while their Italian counterparts brought Nebbiolo, Sangiovese, Barbera, and Bonarda. The Mendoza region produces more than two-thirds of the country's wine, and probably a larger proportion of the exported wine. The region's higher western parts generally produce the best wines – some labels give the altitude of the vineyards.

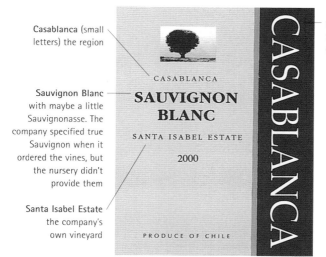

Casablanca (small letters) the region

Casablanca (big letters) the producer – rather confusing, I know

Sauvignon Blanc with maybe a little Sauvignonasse. The company specified true Sauvignon when it ordered the vines, but the nursery didn't provide them

Santa Isabel Estate the company's own vineyard

Fabre e Montmayou French-inspired producer

Malbec Argentina's trump-card grape

Luján de Cuyo classy red wine district of Mendoza

Vino Fino Tinto fine red wine (which it is)

All of the major wine-producing countries in Europe, and almost all of the minor ones, are members of the European Union (EU). There are certain wine-labelling laws common to all EU countries, plus others that are country-specific. The most important EU-wide regulation concerns a wine's identity, so the label must state whether it is a table wine, a quality wine, or a wine from an intermediate level. A quality wine is sometimes indicated by the letters VQPRD (*vin de qualité produit dans une région déterminée*, or quality wine from a designated area). However, most countries have their own translations of the categories, as the table below shows. Further explanations of the terms can be found in the country entries (*see* pages 26–58).

# europe

|  | Table wine | Regional wine | Quality wine | Superior quality wine |
|---|---|---|---|---|
| France | *vin de table* | *vin de pays* | VDQS | AC/AOC |
| Germany | *tafelwein* | *landwein* | QbA | QmP |
| Italy | *vino da tavola* | IGT | DOC | DOCG |
| Portugal | *vinho de mesa* | *vinho regional* | IPR | DOC |
| Spain | *vino de mesa* | *vino de la tierra* | DO | DOCa |

Labels for table wines must make no mention of grape variety/ies, vintage or place of origin. The further you travel up the identity ladder from table wines (the further right you move in this table, in other words), the more precise the rules

are governing a wine's provenance, permitted grape
varieties, and methods of production.

In theory, the quality should also be higher, but this
isn't always the case. The appellation laws were originally
drawn up to prevent fraud, but many quality-minded
producers now find them something of a straitjacket.
As a result, some choose to take a step down the identity
ladder in order to enjoy greater freedom in blending. For
example, many *appellations contrôlées* (ACs) in southern
France forbid the use of Cabernet Sauvignon. Producers
who wish to add some Cabernet simply label their wine
as *vin de pays*. For a European wine of genuine "quality",
the name of the producer is at least as important as
which tier of the quality ladder it comes from.

### Ancient and modern

Two world-class wines.
One is a classic from Ribera
del Duero – its label would
not have looked out of
place a century ago. The
other is a splendid and
strikingly labelled Pouilly-
Fumé from one of the
world's finest exponents
of Sauvignon Blanc.

VEGA-SICILIA

*RESERVA ESPECIAL* "UNICO"

**Ribera del Duero**

Denominación de Origen

Medalla de Oro y Gran Diploma de Honor
Feria de Navidad de Madrid de 1927
Medalla de Oro y Gran Diploma de Honor
Exposición Hotelera de Barcelona de 1927
Gran Premio de Honor
Exposición Internacional de Barcelona 1929-30

75Cl.                    13.5% Vol.

EMBOTELLADO EN LA PROPIEDAD
BODEGAS VEGA SICILIA, S. A.    VALBUENA DE DUERO (Valladolid) España

Hemos seleccionado para su venta 40 barricas de
nuestras mejores reservas que hacen un total de
11.640 botellas.

El número de esta botella es el

BODEGAS VEGA SICILIA, S. A.
El Presidente

RIBERA DEL DUERO TABLE WINE              PRODUCT OF SPAIN
IMPORTED BY: PRESTIGE WINE CORP. – NEW YORK, NEW YORK
SHIPPED BY: EUROPVIN – CHRISTOPHER CANNAN
CONTAINS SULFITES              ALC. 13,5% BY VOL. – 750 ML

1988                              N° embldor. 2342

DIDIER DAGUENEAU

EN CHAILLOUX

Alsace is unusual in France in that most of the AC wines are labelled according to grape variety. Champagne is AC, but such is its reputation that the words don't appear on the label.

# alsace & champagne

### Alsace

While some AC varieties appear elsewhere in France, others are confined to Alsace, and one, Klevener de Heiligenstein, is found only in a small district in northern Alsace. Blends can be labelled *gentil* or *edelzwicker*. Vineyard names appear on some labels and if the vineyard is one of the fifty *grand cru* sites, the appellation will be Alsace Grand Cru. Such *grand cru* wines can only be made from Riesling, Pinot Gris, Muscat, or Gewurztraminer.

### Champagne

Vintage Champagne states a date on its bottle, but non vintage shows no year. Blanc de blancs is made entirely from Chardonnay, and blanc de noirs from Pinot Meunier and/or Pinot Noir. The scale for Champagne runs (from driest to sweetest): brut nature; extra brut; brut; extra dry or extra sec, dry or *sec*; rich or *demi-sec*, and *doux*.

Small initials on the label indicate the type of producer: RM (a grower); NM (a producer who buys in grapes); CM (a cooperative of growers), and MA (a supermarket or wine merchant's brand name). The numbers that follow these initials identify the producer.

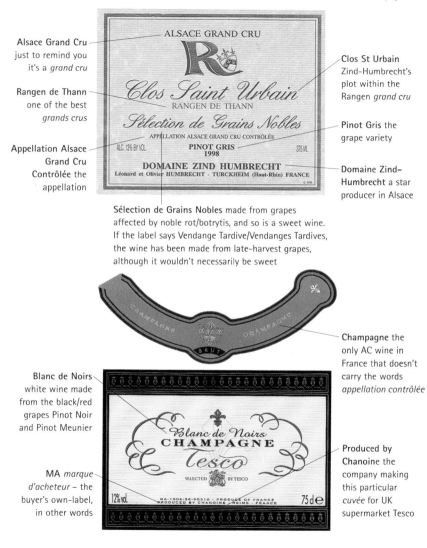

**Alsace Grand Cru** just to remind you it's a *grand cru*

**Rangen de Thann** one of the best *grands crus*

**Appellation Alsace Grand Cru Contrôlée** the appellation

ALSACE GRAND CRU

*Clos Saint Urbain*

RANGEN DE THANN

*Sélection de Grains Nobles*

APPELLATION ALSACE GRAND CRU CONTRÔLÉE

ALC. 13% BY VOL | PINOT GRIS 1998 | 375 ML

**DOMAINE ZIND HUMBRECHT**
Léonard et Olivier HUMBRECHT - TURCKHEIM (Haut-Rhin) FRANCE

L 458

**Clos St Urbain** Zind-Humbrecht's plot within the Rangen *grand cru*

**Pinot Gris** the grape variety

**Domaine Zind-Humbrecht** a star producer in Alsace

**Sélection de Grains Nobles** made from grapes affected by noble rot/botrytis, and so is a sweet wine. If the label says Vendange Tardive/Vendanges Tardives, the wine has been made from late-harvest grapes, although it wouldn't necessarily be sweet

CHAMPAGNE CHAMPAGNE BRUT

**Champagne** the only AC wine in France that doesn't carry the words *appellation contrôlée*

**Blanc de Noirs** white wine made from the black/red grapes Pinot Noir and Pinot Meunier

*Blanc de Noirs*
**CHAMPAGNE**
*Tesco*

SELECTED BY TESCO

12% vol. | MA-1904-56-00310 - PRODUCE OF FRANCE "PRODUCED BY CHANOINE - REIMS - FRANCE | 75 d e

**Produced by Chanoine** the company making this particular *cuvée* for UK supermarket Tesco

**MA** *marque d'acheteur* – the buyer's own-label, in other words

The Burgundians label their wines according to a hierarchy
of vineyard sites developed over several centuries.

# burgundy

At the bottom of the quality ladder are the so-called
generic appellations, such Bourgogne Rouge and Crémant
de Bourgogne, that can come from anywhere within the
Burgundy region. Then come the village wines –
Marsannay, Mercurey, and so on. Sometimes the vineyard
will be shown on the label – Meursault Les Tillets, for
example – but unless the words *premier cru* or *1er cru*
appear, this is simply a *lieu-dit*, or named site.

Next are the *premiers crus*, vineyards considered
superior to the regular village sites. The labels bear the
village name, the *premier cru* designation, and sometimes
the vineyard name - Chablis Premier Cru Fourchaume,
Chassagne-Montrachet Premier Cru La Maltroie. If the
label simply says Nuits-St-Georges Premier Cru, then the
wine is a blend from *premier cru* vineyards.

Finally, the *grands crus*, whose labels make no mention
of the village name. So while you might guess that Le
Musigny is in Chambolle-Musigny, you'll need a wine
book to discover that La Tâche lies in Vosne-Romanée.

Got all that? Unfortunately, the majority of vineyards
have more than one owner. There isn't just one Clos
Vougeot made each year, there are dozens. How can you
tell from the label which is a good example, and which is
a bad one? You can't. Ah well, that's burgundy.

Appellation Musigny Contrôlée could also say *appellation grand cru contrôlée* or simply *appellation contrôlée*

Musigny name of the vineyard

Grand Cru required on all *grand cru* wines

Réserve Numérotée the bottles are all numbered at de Vogüé. This is a sample label, hence the number is missing

Vieilles Vignes old vines. There's no limit on how *vieille* a *vigne* has to be for such a term to be used

Mis en Bouteille au Domaine bottled at the estate

Domaine Comte Georges de Vogüé one of the top growers in Burgundy, and owner of more than half of the Musigny Grand Cru

Cru du Beaujolais ten villages in the Beaujolais region are deemed to be of a higher standard than basic beaujolais

Appellation Brouilly Contrôlée it's beaujolais, but because it's from one of the ten *crus*, the label doesn't have to say so

Mis en Bouteille par Les Vins Georges Dubœuf bottled by Georges Dubœuf, the most important beaujolais producer, even if he doesn't have any vineyards of his own

After the intricacies of Burgundy, Bordeaux is a little simpler to comprehend. The typical estate often makes just one wine from one appellation. In a bid to enhance the quality of this wine, some châteaux (the word château has no quality connotations) select only the best batches of wine for the *grand vin*. The remainder is then released as a "second wine" – Les Forts de Latour from Château Latour is an example of this. Some producers even produce a third tier of quality.

# bordeaux

There are also fewer appellations than in Burgundy. The generic ACs are the base level, with the main ones being Bordeaux and Bordeaux Supérieur – the term Supérieur indicates a slightly higher alcohol level. Then come some more precisely defined regions – Blaye, Bourg, Médoc, Entre-Deux-Mers, Graves, Sauternes, St-Emilion, Pomerol, and so on. Some are further divided: top Graves wines usually come from Pessac-Léognan; top Médoc reds from Margaux, Pauillac, St-Estèphe, and St-Julien.

Cabernet Sauvignon, Cabernet Franc, and Merlot are red Bordeaux's main grapes, with Malbec and Petit Verdot giving occasional support. Merlot dominates, but in the Graves and Médoc, Cabernet Sauvignon has the upper hand. Bordeaux whites are made mostly from Sauvignon Blanc and Sémillon, with perhaps a little Muscadelle.

Rather than remember vineyard hierarchies, Bordeaux fans must acquaint themselves with classifications of châteaux. The most famous, the 1855 classification,

divided the top red wines of the region into five tiers –
*premier grand cru classé* or First Growth; *deuxième grand
cru classé* or Second Growth, and so on.

Bordeaux whites were also classified and everything
on the list came from Sauternes or its neighbour Barsac.
The three tiers are *premier cru supérieur* (Château
d'Yquem is the only one), *premier cru,* and *deuxième cru.*

Today, the regions of St-Emilion and Graves both have
their own classifications, and there is also a classification
of the *crus bourgeois* of the Médoc, that grades those
properties that are not included in the 1855 list. These
classifications are extensive and, on occasion, also
controversial, and the comparative price of a wine is
often as good an indication of quality as any ranking.

Appellation
St-Emilion Grand
Cru Contrôlée
the *appellation
contrôlée* name

Famille Vauthier
the Vauthier family
owns a number of
châteaux in Bordeaux

**CHATEAU AUSONE**

**1ᵉʳ GRAND CRU CLASSÉ
SAINT-EMILION GRAND CRU**

APPELLATION SAINT-ÉMILION GRAND CRU CONTRÔLÉE

**1997**

*Famille VAUTHIER*
PROPRIÉTAIRE A SAINT-ÉMILION (GIRONDE) FRANCE

Alc. 12,5% vol.  MIS EN BOUTEILLE AU CHATEAU    750 ml
DÉPOSE            PRODUIT DE FRANCE - BORDEAUX        L 1

Château Ausone
first-class producer

1er Grand Cru Classé
could say *premier grand
cru classé* "A" because
Ausone (along with
Cheval Blanc) is
considered superior to
other *premier grands
crus classés.* The levels
below this are *grand
cru classé, grand cru,*
and plain St-Emilion

France's longest river, the Loire, is very much white wine territory. The country's other great wine river, the Rhône, is dominated by reds.

# the loire & rhône valleys

### The Loire Valley

East of the mouth of the Loire River is Muscadet. More than eighty per cent of the region's wines come from the Sèvre and Maine sub-region (the other sub-regions are Coteaux de la Loire and Côtes de Grandlieu), and all use the Melon de Bourgogne grape. The best are labelled sur lie to show they've been aged on the lees. Cabernets Sauvignon and Franc are used for most Loire reds, and Gamay also appears. Sancerre and Pouilly-Fumé are best known for whites made from Sauvignon Blanc, while Chenin Blanc dominates Anjou-Saumur and Touraine.

### The Rhône Valley

In the north, the red wines of Côte-Rôtie, Hermitage, Cornas, Crozes-Hermitage, and St-Joseph are usually 100 per cent Syrah; whites are either 100 per cent Viognier or Marsanne/Roussanne blends. Further south, whites tend to be blends of these three grapes plus Grenache Blanc. Over a dozen red varieties are permitted for Châteauneuf-du-Pape, Lirac, Gigondas, and Vacqueyras, though they tend to be Grenache based. Most Côtes du Rhône also comes from the Southern Rhône and word villages indicates vineyards of higher quality.

Le Mont name of the vineyard

Moelleux sweet

Première Trie the pickers make a number of "tries" through the vineyard to select the ripest, sweetest grapes. The best grapes come from the first trie

Vouvray the appellation

Huet the finest producer of Vouvray

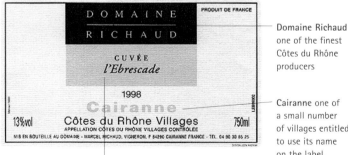

Domaine Richaud one of the finest Côtes du Rhône producers

Cairanne one of a small number of villages entitled to use its name on the label. The appellation remains Côtes du Rhône Villages

Cuvée l'Ebrescade grape varieties are forbidden on Rhône labels, so this is how Marcel Richaud labels his wine, a blend of Grenache, Syrah, and Mourvèdre from one of his top vineyards

Southern France has a number of ACs covering vineyards from the Italian border in Provence to the Spanish border in Roussillon. But only a small proportion of the vast quantity of wine made qualifies for an AC. A significant (although declining) amount of rather basic *vin de table* is produced, but more importantly, there is plenty of *vin de pays*.

# southern france

With *vins de pays* the regulations are less strict than for AC, so producers can use a far wider selection of grape varieties, plus put their names on the labels. As a result, the range in quality and style is vast, but the grape varieties and the price of the bottle usually provide some indication of what to expect. Wines labelled *fûts de chêne* have been aged in oak barrels. They are more expensive than regular bottlings, but are not always better.

Geographically, *vin de pays* fall into three tiers. First are four regions: Jardin de la France, covering the Loire; Comté Tolosan, covering southwest France; Comtés Rhodaniens, covering central and eastern France; and Oc, covering Languedoc-Roussillon. Then there are the winemaking *départements*, and finally there are almost 100 local designations, though many producers bypass these, and use either the departmental or regional names.

The south is also home to most of France's *vins doux naturels* (VDN), made by adding spirit to a semi-fermented wine, leaving a fortified wine with some residual sugar. Look out for Muscat de Rivesaltes, Maury, and Banyuls.

Clos l'Angely a single vineyard wine

**DOMAINE PICCININI** — Domaine Piccinini a consistent performer in Minervois

Clos l'Angély

1998

MINERVOIS-LA LIVINIÈRE — Minervois–La Livinière the best sub-region of Minervois

*APPELLATION MINERVOIS-LA LIVINIÈRE CONTRÔLÉE*

*MIS EN BOUTEILLE À F 11160*
*PAR J.C. PICCININI, ARTISAN-VIGNERON*
*34210 - LA LIVINIÈRE - FRANCE*
*TÉL. 04 68 91 44 32*
*PRODUIT DE FRANCE*

12,5% vol.
e 750 ml

**· LA BAUME ·**

2 0       0 1

**SAUVIGNON BLANC**

TROPICAL FRUIT INTENSITY ·
LIGHTLY HERBACEOUS · CRISP
AND DRY · SERVE CHILLED

La Baume Sauvignon Blanc a clean simple label that will appeal to those reared on New World wines. All the legal requirements appear on the back label (*see* page 60)

For many, the northwest of Italy means Nebbiolo, the grape responsible for the majestic reds of Barolo and Barbaresco.

# northwest italy

Barolo and Barbaresco were among Italy's first wines to be classed *denominazione di origine controllata e garantita* (DOCG). Neither DOCG is divided into official zones, but many growers choose to mention a particular vineyard (the words *vigneto, sorì* or *bricco* are sometimes used) on the label. Both are 100 per cent Nebbiolo. Those choosing to blend in other varieties use a more general DOC (DOCG without the guarantee), such as DOC Langhe. Nebbiolo performs less well outside Barolo and Barbaresco, but it makes decent wines under the Nebbiolo d'Alba and Roero DOCs, as well as DOCG Gattinara, and DOC Ghemme in northern Piedmont, where Nebbiolo is called Spanna.

Piedmont's other main red grapes are Barbera and Dolcetto, both of which are being treated with increased respect, particularly in the DOCs of Dolcetto di Dogliani, Dolcetto d'Alba, Barbera d'Alba, and Barbera d'Asti. Piedmont has remained immune to the influx of IGTs (*indicazione geografica tipica - see* page 40), and there is a province-wide DOC Piemonte (the Italian for Piedmont) to cover wines that don't fit into other appellations.

Asti is more famous for its eponymous DOCG sparkling wine (the *spumante* has now been dropped) made from Muscat. Another white Piedmont DOCG is Cortese di Gavi or - if it is made close to the town of Gavi - Gavi de Gavi. Look out too, for wines made from the nutty Arneis grape.

But Asti is not the only sparkling wine of repute in northwest Italy. In Lombardy, the Franciacorta DOCG includes some world-class *metodo classico/tradizionale* (traditional method) wines made from Chardonnay, Pinot Blanc, Pinot Gris, and Pinot Noir. The often excellent table wines of the region come under the Terre de Franciacorta DOC. To the east, Lugana DOC is a rare outpost of quality for Trebbiano. Nebbiolo is grown in northern Lombardy, where Valtellina Superiore is DOCG. Versions made from dried grapes are labelled *sfurzat/sforzato*.

**Bric dël Fiasc** Piemontese dialect for the Bricco Fiasco vineyard, one of Barolo's finest

**Imbottigliato** helpfully translated on the label

**Non desperdere il vetro nell'ambiente** dispose of the bottle thoughtfully, in other words

The regions of Friuli-Venezia Giulia and Trentino-Alto Adige
use varietal labelling. Look out for Soave and Valpolicella in
Veneto, while Emilia-Romagna's claim to fame is Lambrusco.

# northeast italy

Friuli-Venezia Giulia produces some of Italy's finest whites
and, increasingly, fine reds in the DOCs of Colli Orientali
del Friuli, Isonzo, Grave del Friuli, and Collio. Varietals are
also popular and the grapes used include familiar names,
such as Chardonnay, and local varieties like Ribolla Gialla.

In Italian-speaking Trentino, many wines come under
the Valdadige or Trentino DOCs, but the Teroldego grape
has its own enclave in DOC Teroldego Rotaliano. Some
local grapes, such as Schiava, are also found further north
in German-speaking Alto Adige (Südtirol). The Germanic
influence means that a wine made from Schiava in the
DOC Lago di Caldaro could appear as DOC Kalterersee.

The Veneto is home to Soave and Valpolicella, and
these are much-abused names, but the wines can be
fabulous, if they come from the *classico* zones (the
historic vineyards of the region). Recioto di Soave (a
DOCG) is made from *passito* grapes, picked super-ripe
then allowed to shrivel over a period of a few months
before vinification. The result is a decadent sweet wine.
Amarone is a version that has been fermented to dryness.

Famed for its Lambrusco, Emilia-Romagna is also
home to Italy's first white DOCG, Albana di Romagna,
with wines ranging from *secco* (dry) to *dolce* (sweet).

Vigneti di Moron a rather unfortunately named single vineyard

**DOMÌNI VENETI®**

1998

*Vigneti di Moron*

RECIOTO della VALPOLICELLA
DENOMINAZIONE DI ORIGINE CONTROLLATA
CLASSICO

DOC curiously, Recioto and its close relative Amarone are not DOCG

**Ronco del Gnemiz®**
colli orientali del Friuli
denominazione di origine controllata
Schioppettino
**1997**
Imbottigliato all'origine dall'azienda agricola
**Ronco del Gnemiz**
società semplice in San Giovanni al Natisone - Italia - Prodotto in Italia
750 ML ℮   L ISO-97   Non disperdere il vetro nell'ambiente   13% VOL

Schioppettino one of a number of intriguing indigenous grapes, this one is red

Colli Orientali del Friuli the local DOC, often abbreviated to COF

Azienda Agricola indicates that the estate makes wine with only its own grapes, often seen as Az Ag

Tuscany boasts a number of DOCGs. Chianti in its various forms, Brunello di Montalcino, Vino Nobile di Montepulciano, and Carmignano are all exclusively, or predominately, Sangiovese, while Vernaccia di San Gimignano is the sole DOCG white. So these are Tuscany's best wines? Not necessarily...

# tuscany & central italy

A revolution began in the 1970s when many producers simply threw out the DOC rule book and concentrated on making the finest wines possible. The only appellation open to these so-called Super Tuscan wines was *vino da tavola* (table wine). So the IGT (*indicazione geografica tipica*) category was introduced, which is similar to the French *vin de pays* category. But it is more useful to remember the best wines/producers than the 100+ IGTs.

DOC Sangioveses to look out for include Rosso di Montalcino and Morellino di Scansano. Other reds of note include Bolgheri (the best-known wine Sassicaia has its own DOC), and Val di Cornia with its Suvereto sub-zone. The *passito* wine, *vin santo*, which is made in several parts of Italy (*see* page 38), is at its best here.

Neighbouring Umbria has an increasingly impressive mix of IGTs and DOCs, along with the DOCG reds of Torgiano and Sagrantino di Montefalco. Orvieto, made from Trebbiano and Malvasia, is the best-known Umbrian white – again, look out for *classico* wines. A similar blend is used in Lazio for the (in)famous Frascati. The state's best wines, usually red, often appear as IGT Lazio.

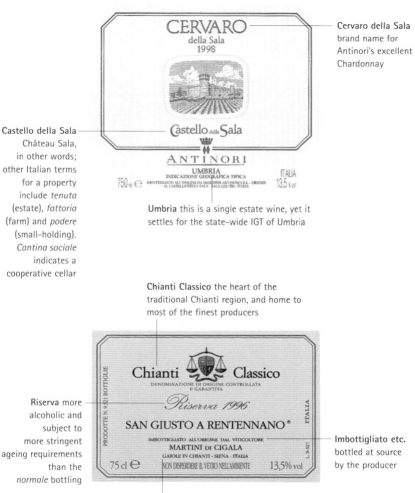

**Cervaro della Sala** brand name for Antinori's excellent Chardonnay

**Castello della Sala** Château Sala, in other words; other Italian terms for a property include *tenuta* (estate), *fattoria* (farm) and *podere* (small-holding). *Cantina sociale* indicates a cooperative cellar

**Umbria** this is a single estate wine, yet it settles for the state-wide IGT of Umbria

**Chianti Classico** the heart of the traditional Chianti region, and home to most of the finest producers

**Riserva** more alcoholic and subject to more stringent ageing requirements than the *normale* bottling

**Imbottigliato etc.** bottled at source by the producer

**Gaiole** important chianti classico village

A region was once simply the source of large volumes
of basic plonk, southern Italy is now continuing the wine
revolution that Tuscany began in the 1970s.

# southern italy & the islands

Southern Italy is undergoing the sort of renaissance that
has transformed southern France in recent years. Upgraded
cellars are working wonders with a healthy mix of familiar
grapes and some fascinating, and often high-class,
indigenous varieties. These include Aglianico, Nero d'Avola,
Uva di Troia, Negroamaro, Primitivo (the same as
California's Zinfandel), Gaglioppo, and Malvasia Nera for
reds, and Greco Bianco and Fiano for whites. Some wines
fit neatly into existing DOCs, but others are content with
an IGT designation. Once again, the name of the producer
and the grape variety are more important than the IGT.

Campania has historically been the source of some
of the south's finest wines, and this tradition continues
with the DOCs of Greco di Tufo, Fiano d'Avellino (both
white), and the Aglianico-based Taurasi, the sole DOCG
red. Basilicata's retort, indeed, its only wine of note, is
Aglianico del Vulture. The toe of the Italian boot, Calabria,
has the Gaglioppo-based Cirò, but it's the heel, the region
of Puglia, where most of the action is taking place. The
majority of the interesting newcomers fall under the IGT
Puglia, but there's also plenty of activity in the DOCs of
Salice Salento, Brindisi (both Negroamaro based), and
Primitivo di Manduria.

Nero d'Avola, either on its own or blended with Cabernet and friends, is behind most of Sicily's best reds, with many of them IGTs rather than DOCs. Marsala, the island's most famous DOC, comes in three colours - *oro* (gold), *ambre* (amber), and *rubino* (ruby). Young wines are sold as *fine*, while those labelled *superiore* and the top-of-the-tree *vergine* (also called *solera*) have to conform to certain ageing requirements. Decent marsala is hard to find, so if you want something for puddings or cheeses, try the superb sweet Moscatos and *passitos* (*see* page 38) from the island of Pantelleria.

Sardinia has a white DOCG with Vermentino di Gallura – the Vendemmia Tardiva or late-harvest versions are the finest. Better still are the Rhône-meets-Italy reds made from Cannonau (Grenache), Carignano (Carignan), and the local grape Monica, as well as the occasional IGT Cabernet.

**Trulli** a venture between the Cantele winery and a UK-based company. Named after the conical stone buildings of the region

**Salento** the name of the IGT

**Zinfandel** some producers label their wines Zinfandel rather than Primitivo because...

The winds of change that have been sweeping through Italy for the past two decades are now blowing in Spain. Producers are not rebelling against the DO (*denominación de origen*) system, but against the country's traditions of blending and ageing wines. This is especially apparent in Rioja.

# rioja & ribera del duero

Rioja is Spain's only DOCa – the Ca is for *calificada*. Tempranillo is the predominant grape variety, aided by Garnacha (Grenache), Mazuelo (Carignan), Graciano, and Cabernet Sauvignon. Viura (Macabeo) dominates white Rioja production. Quality levels for Rioja (and most Spanish wines) are based on the length of ageing. A wine aged for at least two years (one in barrel, one in bottle) is labelled *crianza*. A *reserva* is three years old (at least one in barrel and one in bottle) and a *gran reserva* must be five years old (at least two in barrel and two in bottle). Traditional Rioja is a blended wine from diverse vineyards, but small production, single-vineyard wines are now being made (the terms *viña* and *viñedo* indicate the vineyard name).

Navarra uses Cabernet Sauvignon, Merlot, Tempranillo, and Garnacha for its reds, and also makes some delicious Garnacha *rosados* (rosés) and tasty Chardonnays, some of which are *fermentado en barrica* (barrel-fermented). As *tinto fino* or *tinto del país*, Tempranillo is also the force behind the highly rated wines of Ribera del Duero. The ladder of *crianza, reserva,* and *gran reserva* exists here too, but, as in Rioja, the name of the bodega is vital.

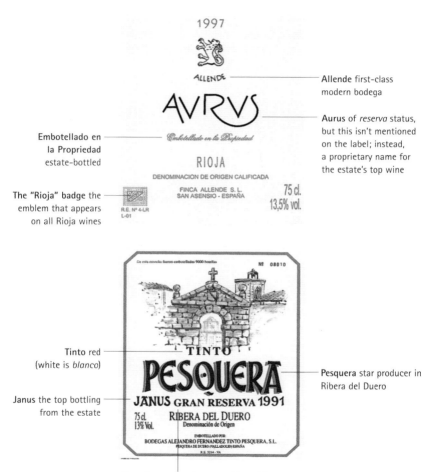

**Allende** first-class modern bodega

**Aurus** of *reserva* status, but this isn't mentioned on the label; instead, a proprietary name for the estate's top wine

**Embotellado en la Propriedad** estate-bottled

The **"Rioja" badge** the emblem that appears on all Rioja wines

**Tinto** red (white is *blanco*)

**Janus** the top bottling from the estate

**Pesquera** star producer in Ribera del Duero

**Gran Reserva** has been aged in oak for at least two years, and had further bottle ageing before release

Where once there was little vinous activity apart from Rioja, northern Spain now teems with activity. The hottest spot is Catalonia, home of cava. Historically it has been made from Parellada, Xarel-lo, and Macabeo grapes, but Chardonnay and Pinot Noir are being increasingly planted.

# northern spain

Successful as cava is, the *vino de mesa* (table wines) of Catalonia today garner most interest. The Priorat region has been making concentrated spicy reds using a combination of old-vine Garnacha and Cariñena (Carignan, unrelated to the DO) since the late 1980s. Priorat is still only a DO, although prices can exceed those of the Rioja DOCa. The varietal wines of Penedès and Costers del Segre, as well as those made to the west in Somontano, are more "international". Decent Catalan whites are hard to find, although some of the rare whites of Priorat, made from obscure local grapes, can impress.

Obscure is also an appropriate word for the rare, but refreshing, whites from Bilbao on the north coast. Another word is unpronounceable – try Chacolí de Vizcaya and Chacolí de Guetaria, or Bizkaiako Txakolina and Getariako Txakolina. Spain's most highly rated white wines can be found in Galicia's Rías Baixas. Many of these are 100 per cent Albariño, but the traditional style is a blend in which the Treixadura and Loureira grapes also play a part.

The pick of the Galician reds are those made from the Mencía grape in Bierzo and Ribeira Sacra.

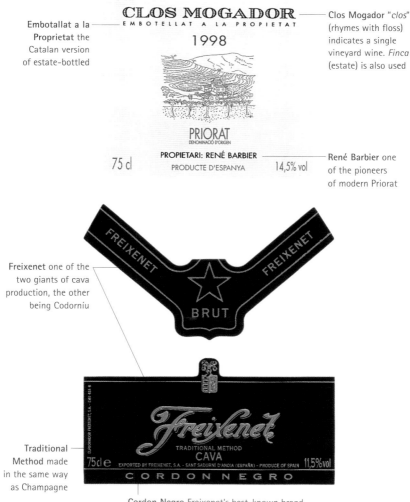

Embotallat a la Proprietat the Catalan version of estate-bottled

**CLOS MOGADOR**
EMBOTELLAT A LA PROPIETAT
1998

PRIORAT
DENOMINACIÓ D'ORIGEN

PROPIETARI: RENÉ BARBIER
PRODUCTE D'ESPANYA

75 cl

14,5% vol

Clos Mogador "*clos*" (rhymes with floss) indicates a single vineyard wine. *Finca* (estate) is also used

René Barbier one of the pioneers of modern Priorat

Freixenet one of the two giants of cava production, the other being Codorniu

FREIXENET

BRUT

*Freixenet*
TRADITIONAL METHOD
CAVA
EXPORTED BY FREIXENET, S.A. - SANT SADURNÍ D'ANOIA (ESPAÑA) - PRODUCE OF SPAIN
C O R D O N   N E G R O

75 cl e

11,5% vol

ELABORADOR FREIXENET, S.A. - E.R.D 464-B

Traditional Method made in the same way as Champagne

Cordon Negro Freixenet's best-known brand

It's a case of quantity rather than quality in southern and central Spain, with the massive DO of La Mancha being the most obvious culprit. However, there are signs of improvement. Growers in Jumilla are exploiting old Monastrell (Mourvèdre) vineyards and making some decent spicy reds.

# central & southern spain

Valencia is enjoying some success with table wines, but is better known as the home of one of the world's best-value dessert wines, Moscatel de Valencia. Finer, but rarer, sweet wines are found on the south coast in Malaga. Various styles are made using Moscatel and Pedro Ximénez (PX), from unfortified *passito* (*see* page 38) to fortified wines similar to the *vins doux naturels* of Roussillon (*see* page 34).

In the sherry vineyards between Seville and Cádiz the dominant grape is Palomino. Here, an intricate blending system called a *solera* transforms neutral base wines into something special. Through the action of a yeasty growth called *flor*, the lightest wines of the region become finos (in Jerez and Puerto de Santa María) and manzanillas (in Sanlúcar). Olorosos are fuller-bodied, while palo cortado sits halfway between these two styles. In amontillados the *flor* has died on a fino, and the wine has continued ageing in barrel, though inferior versions are sweetened olorosos. Cream and pale cream sherries have a similar origin. The finest sweet sherries are olorosos bolstered by some *passito*-style PX, and a few bodegas even make superb, raisiny wine exclusively from PX.

**Manzanilla Pasada** a manzanilla where the *flor* has died and the wine has continued ageing. Fino amontillado is its equivalent

**Hidalgo** the great name of manzanilla

**Pastrana** a rare single-vineyard sherry from the Pastrana vineyard. Most sherries are blends from a variety of *almacenistas* – the stockholders who provide wines for the bodegas to age

**Castillo de Liria** a brand of Gandia, the most important producer of Moscatel de Valencia

**V.L.C.P.R.D. Quality Liqueur Wine PSR** a *vin doux naturel*

**Dessert Wine/ Vin Doux** the label includes French translations of several terms

German wine labels are an example of a desire to provide information taken too far. Everything you could possibly wish to know about the location of the producer and vineyard, place of bottling, and the district where the wine was officially tested is on there somewhere, either in words or codified in the AP (*Amtliche Prüfungsnummer*) number. What the label won't tell you, however, is the quality of the wine.

# germany

The definition of the word "quality" is stretched to extremes in Germany, where ninety-five per cent of the wine produced qualifies as "quality wine" (the rest is *tafelwein* or *landwein* – see page 24). There are two tiers here: QbA (*Qualitätswein bestimmter Anbaugebiete*) and QmP (*Qualitätswein mit Prädikat*). A QbA might be a fine Riesling from a top estate or an insipid, sickly Liebfraumilch. The price usually tells you what to expect.

QmP wines are categorized according to the must weights (sugar levels) of the grapes at harvest. The basis for this method is that the best vineyards will produce the ripest, sweetest, and therefore best, grapes. The idea falls down with grape varieties that have been developed for easy ripening in the marginal conditions of some German vineyards. The must weights might be high, but the quality often isn't.

The levels in the *Prädikat* system are: Kabinett; then Spätlese (late-picked), Auslese (selected bunches), Beerenauslese (selected grapes), and Trockenbeerenauslese (selected grapes that have been shrivelled by noble rot).

For each level, there is a minimum must weight, dependent on the region and grape variety. Some growers make wines from grapes that have been left on the vine until the grapes freeze. Providing the must weight is at least of Beerenauslese level, they can be called Eiswein.

Mosel-Saar-Ruwer is best known for its delicate, racy Rieslings. Don't be surprised to see alcohol levels as low as seven and a half per cent. This is close to the northern limit of viticulture, and the acidity level in the grapes is high. To balance this, growers often stop the fermentation before all the sugar has turned to alcohol. But more on this over the page.

Erdener from the village of Erden

Prälat the name of the vineyard

Riesling made from the Riesling grape

Auslese the *Prädikat* level

8.0% a low level, meaning the wine will have some residual sugar

Dr Loosen a dynamic grower

Mosel-Saar-Ruwer the region of origin

It's warmer in the Rheingau than in the Mosel-Saar-Ruwer and, as a result, potential alcohol levels are higher while acidity is lower. With less need for residual sugar in the wines, the tendency today is to make *halbtrocken* (medium-dry) or *trocken* (dry) wines. Sweet wines are usually made solely from grapes affected by noble rot.

Several growers still bottle a number of wines at different *Prädikat* levels from the same vineyard, with some even producing three or four different bottlings of the same quality. They can use the number of a cask (*fuder*), a gold capsule (*goldkapsel*), or better still a long gold capsule (*lange goldkapsel*) over the cork to distinguish between them.

There is also a move among growers only to highlight their best vineyard sites - *erstes gewächs* (first growth) or *erstes gewächs* (great growth) depending on the region – on bottles. Wines from lesser vineyards are used in blends labelled varietally, with *Prädikat* level and the grower's name. Another effort to simplify German labels is the introduction of Classic and Selection wines. These are dry varietal wines that meet certain ripeness and quality criteria, with Selection being the higher level.

Riesling is Germany's main, but not only, quality grape. Scheurebe, Silvaner, Rieslaner, and Gewürztraminer can all be excellent, as can wines made from members of the Pinot family – Pinot Blanc (Weisser Burgunder), Pinot Gris (Grauburgunder), and Pinot Noir (Spätburgunder). Some of the Spätburgunders are world-class, although many can only claim QbA status because they have been chaptalized (had sugar added to boost the alcohol level).

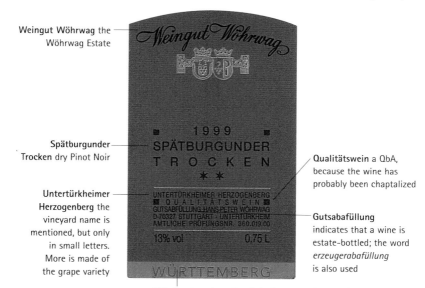

**Weingut Wöhrwag** the Wöhrwag Estate

**Spätburgunder Trocken** dry Pinot Noir

**Untertürkheimer Herzogenberg** the vineyard name is mentioned, but only in small letters. More is made of the grape variety

**Qualitätswein** a QbA, because the wine has probably been chaptalized

**Gutsabafüllung** indicates that a wine is estate-bottled; the word *erzeugerabafüllung* is also used

**Württemberg** large but little-known region, specializing in red wines

**Georg Breuer** leading Rheingau producer of great wines with simple, stylish labels

**Rüdesheim** the town

**Berg Schlossberg** the vineyard

**The three arches** is the unofficial symbol for Rheingau growers indicating an *erstes gewächs* wine (all of which are dry)

Portugal's best-known wine is port. It comes in many forms, including white, but falls into two broad types, ruby and tawny.

# northern portugal

Ruby port is a blend from recent vintages. Vintage port is a wine from a good vintage that has spent two to three years in barrel before being bottled. Late-bottled vintage (LBV) spends up to six years in barrel. Some wines, labelled "traditional", will continue to age in bottle after release. Vintage character is simply a higher quality port.

Tawny ports spend much longer in barrels, "breathing" through the sides of the cask and acquiring their tawny hue. Superior tawnies often carry an indication of their age. A tawny from a single vintage is called a *colheita*.

Table wines (*vinho da mesa*) of the Douro can also be excellent. Most are blends, but varietal bottlings – Touriga Nacional, in particular – are increasing. Most come under the Douro DOC (*denominaçao de origem controlada*), but some come under the *vinho regional* (VR) of Trás-os-Montes.

The other two noteworthy red regions in the north are Bairrada, with wine made mostly from the thick-skinned Baga grape, and Dão, made from a cocktail of varieties, although varietal versions do exist. Bottles labelled *garrafeira* indicate a producer's special reserve bottling.

Northern Portugal is also home to Vinho Verde – Verde meaning "young", not "green". While nearly half the output is red (*tinto*), the crisp white (*branco*) versions are the ones most commonly seen outside the country.

Niepoort small,
high-class family firm

Porto port doesn't have to
mention that it is DOC

Colheita a vintage-dated
tawny. The label shows
that it has spent nearly
fourteen years in barrel
before bottling

Luis Pato Pato (his
surname means
duck, hence the label)
is arguably Bairrada's
finest producer

Vinha Barrosa a wine from
the Barrosa vineyard

Vinha Velha old vines

Criado e Engarrafado par
"produced and bottled by"

Port isn't Portugal's only great fortified wine. Off the coast of Africa lies Madeira and its famous eponymous wine. Most is made from the undistinguished Tinta Negra Mole grape.

# southern portugal

Madeira wines can only be labelled according to their average age – 3 year old, 5 year old, and so on – and their sweetness level – dry, medium-dry, medium-sweet, rich or sweet. The richest and sweetest is malmsey (Malvasia), then comes bual, verdelho, and finally the searing sercial. Most wines are blends of different vintages, although vintage Madeira can be found. This has spent a minimum of twenty years in cask. Some vintage wines that have had less cask age are bottled as *colheitas*.

A less famous fortified wine is the Moscatel made on the Setúbal Peninsula, southeast of Lisbon. Most is bottled after four years, but some superb *cuvées* receive much longer ageing. The table wines from regions around Lisbon can be good. Reds are often based on the Periquita grape, while the fine white Bucelas is based on citrusy Arinto. Wines using non-Portuguese grapes appear as VR (*vinho regional*) rather than DOC. There is also a category called IPR (*indicação de proveniencia regulamentada*).

But the real hotbed of activity is the Alentejo. Here the name of the VR or DOC is of far less importance than the producer. Much of the wine comes from large cooperative cellars (*adegas*), but this is also home to some of Portugal's finest and most forward-looking small estates.

Cossart Gordon established producer now owned by the Symington port dynasty

5 year old not precisely five years old, but has the flavour profile expected of a 5 year old wine

Sercial the driest style of madeira

Mouchão splendid wine from the Herdade (estate) de Mouchão

Vinho Regional Alentejano this is very much Mouchão first, Alentejano second

The 1901 logo one of the oldest estates in the region, although the rise in its wine fortunes dates from the mid-1980s

# other european countries

## Austria

Wines use a classification similar to the German scale from Kabinett up to Trockenbeerenauslese and Eiswein, but with an extra category called Ausbruch, which falls between Beerenauslese and Trockenbeerenauslese in terms of sweetness. Wachau has its own three-tier scale for dry Rieslings and Grüner Veltliners. The lightest wines are Steinfeder, then comes Federspiel and finally Smaragd. Other unusual terms you may come across on Austrian labels include *ried* (vineyard), *alte reben* (old vines), Morillon (Chardonnay), Sämling 88 (Scheurebe), and *schilfwein* (a *passito* style, see page 38).

## Hungary

Hungary's most important contribution to the world of wine is Tokaji or Tokay (Tokaj is the name of the region). The bulk of the wine is szamarodni, meaning "as it comes", but dry (*száraz*) and sweet (*edes*) versions exist. But the real glories are the sweet *aszú* wines. *Aszú* is a sticky paste made from ultra-ripe grapes, and the wines are graded according to how much of this is in the blend. The sweetness is measured in *puttonyos* – literally "buckets" – and the more *puttonyos*, the sweeter the wine. A wine labelled *aszú eszencia* is a seven or eight *puttonyos* wine. There is also a classification of the region's vineyards with First, Second, and Third Growth sites, and three Great First Growths.

Grüner Veltliner
speciality of the region

Smaragd must have a
minimum alcohol
level of twelve per
cent; this qualifies
with ease

Rudi Pichler one of
a number of Pichlers
in the Wachau

Wösendorfer
Hochrain the Hochrain
vineyard in the town
of Wösendorf

Tokaji Aszú 6
puttonyos *aszú*
wines have to be a
minimum of three
*puttonyos*; this wine
will be sumptuously
sweet, although
not as sweet as
*aszú eszencia*

Szepsy for many the
finest grower in Tokaj

Where once the backs of bottles were bare, today many, especially from the New World, bear a second label with further details about the wine and its producer.

# the rise of the back label

The information varies in terms of its usefulness. A potted history of the producer can be entertaining, but it's not essential. More helpful are items such as which grape varieties are used, a tasting note, and an indication of how long the wine can be kept. Some labels list winemaking minutiae, such as the picking dates; the sugar level of the grapes at harvest; the source of the wood for the barrels, etc. This can be intimidating, as can serving suggestions that are too precise – "ideal with wind-dried duck on a tomato and tarragon salsa". But some general food ideas are helpful if you're unfamiliar with the style of a wine.

With two labels, producers also have more options for artistic creativity. Information such as the volume, alcohol level, place of origin, and the name and address of the producer or bottler, has to appear on the front label. But legal niceties don't prompt someone to pick a bottle off the shelf – a striking image or name is far more effective. So many wines now have one label with all the legal bumpf, and another with less clutter and more impact. While the first may be the official front label, it's the second that will appear face-forward on the shelf.

**Bonny Doon Cardinal Zin** a classic and witty example of the front-is-back syndrome; the "front" label is the one bearing all the legal requirements plus some prose from Randall Grahm (see pages 62–3)

It is a CARDINAL ZIN to be inordinately PROUD of this WILDLY SPICY, FULL BODIED PAEAN to little red fruit, the ENVY of those WHO TRY, and FAIL. We anticipate its GREEDY acquisition by consumers LUSTING for a COMPLETE GLUTTONOUS, SORRY, that SUPERSONIC GASTRONOMIC EXPERIENCE. This WINE will complement all MANNER of GAME and OTHER WILD BEASTS, including SLOTH. Yr. R Ranger

2001 CALIFORNIA ZINFANDEL
PRODUCED & BOTTLED BY BONNY DOON VINEYARD®
SANTA CRUZ, CA · ALC. 13.7% BY VOL.
www.bonnydoonvineyard.com

GOVERNMENT WARNING: (1) ACCORDING TO THE SURGEON GENERAL, WOMEN SHOULD NOT DRINK ALCOHOLIC BEVERAGES DURING PREGNANCY BECAUSE OF THE RISK OF BIRTH DEFECTS. (2) CONSUMPTION OF ALCOHOLIC BEVERAGES IMPAIRS YOUR ABILITY TO DRIVE A CAR OR OPERATE MACHINERY, AND MAY CAUSE HEALTH PROBLEMS.
CONTAINS SULFITES

2001 BONNY DOON VINEYARD® BEASTLY OLD VINES CARDINAL ZIN

But it's the Ralph Steadman cartoon, and the witty name, that will catch the customer's eye; this wine was banned in the state of Ohio on religious grounds

"Real emetic fans will also go for a 'Hobart Muddy', and a prize-winning 'Cuiver Reserve Château Bottled Nuits St Wagga Wagga', which has a bouquet like an aborigine's armpit." The Monty Python Australian wine sketch might have seemed far-fetched back in the 1970s, however, today's shelves hold wines whose names aren't that far removed from "Château Chunder".

# funny labels

For instance, there's Marilyn Merlot from Napa Valley, with a different picture of Norma Jean for each vintage. There's a New Zealand Sauvignon Blanc called Cat's Pee on a Gooseberry Bush – that's the classic tasting note after all. A pair of wines from the Californian producer Topolos are called Stu Pedasso and Rae Jean Beach (say them quickly to get the full effect). From southern France, there's a similar pair called Old Git and Old Tart. Gimmicks? Maybe, but those who have seen such wines won't forget them. And they're no more of a gimmick than wines using the name of various creeks, peaks, ridges, and bridges. Even if these places exist, they often have little geographical connection to the wine. There is a Jacob's Creek in Australia's Barossa Valley, but most of the wine with that name is from a totally different region. King of the quirky label is Randall Grahm of Bonny Doon Vineyards, California. It can be hard to fully understand the allusions, but the wines have entertaining packaging (see page 61). Where Grahm scores is that his wines are as interesting as his labels.

**Bonny Doon Old Telegram** Randall Grahm's Mataro alludes to Domaine du Vieux Télégraphe in Châteauneuf-du-Pape. Grahm also has a Châteauneuf-styled wine called Le Cigare Volant (Flying Saucer), so called because the local council in Châteauneuf once issued a decree banning flying saucers from landing in the vineyards

## OLD TELEGRAM

FROM BONNY DOON VINEYARD

RE 2000 CALIFORNIA MATARO (MOURVEDRE)

GRAPE OF COTE DE PROVENCE AND SOUTHERN RHONE E G BANDOL STOP

IN AMERICAS AND ESPANA ALSO CALLED MATARO STOP SPICY

PEPPERY MEATY WILDLY AROMATIC CHARACTER STOP WELL SUITED TO

FLAVORFUL FOODS STOP WHEN SEE ON SHELF OR WINELIST STOP

THIS CORRESPONDENT WOULD WRITE MORE STRAIGHTFORWARD LABEL

COPY BUT SUFFERS FROM ADVANCED ETIQUETTORHEA CANT STOP

PRODUCED & BOTTLED BY BONNY DOON VINEYARD
SANTA CRUZ, CA USA • ALCOHOL 14.2% BY VOL

THE WINES OF CHARLES BACK

**Goat-Roti**

2001

14,0% vol    SOUTH AFRICA    ℮0.75ℓ

**Fairview Goat-Rotí** Charles Back's winery in Paarl is home to both goats and vines – the estate is also a major producer of cheese. The goat theme continues with Goats do Roam and Goat d'Afrique. Sadly, some producers in France's Rhône valley fail to be impressed by Back's labels, and are contemplating legal action

# index